IMAGES
of America

CAMP TYSON

On the Cover: Everyone loves a parade, especially when they're seeing things they've never seen before—like the barrage balloons that were unique to the Camp Tyson Barrage Balloon Training Facility in Paris, Tennessee. The little boy on the bicycle was one of hundreds lining the streets to see these Camp Tyson soldiers and their balloons parade through downtown Paris. (Courtesy of Wayne Webb.)

IMAGES
of America

CAMP TYSON

Shannon McFarlin

ARCADIA
PUBLISHING

ISBN 978-1-4671-2427-0

Published by Arcadia Publishing
Charleston, South Carolina

Printed in the United States of America

Library of Congress Control Number: 2016939199

For all general information, please contact Arcadia Publishing:
Telephone 843-853-2070
Fax 843-853-0044
E-mail sales@arcadiapublishing.com
For customer service and orders:
Toll-Free 1-888-313-2665

Visit us on the Internet at www.arcadiapublishing.com

To my mother, grandmother, and great-grandmother, whose stories about Camp Tyson ignited my imagination as a young girl.

Contents

ACKNOWLEDGMENTS

That so many people from Paris and Henry County, Tennessee, have kept their memories of Camp Tyson alive and have kept mementoes from there all these many years is a testament to how important the camp was in their lives. I want to thank all of those people who have shared with me their memories, old photographs, and other mementoes from Camp Tyson.

I especially want to thank Wayne Webb of Mansfield, Tennessee, who had the foresight to attend the Camp Tyson soldiers' reunions and make copies of the photographs they brought with them. Without Webb, many of those photographs would have been lost over time.

I also want to thank the Carothers family, the employees at the Lhoist Spinks Clay Company, and the late Rebecca Goins, who shared with me their photograph albums and old records so that I could have a complete picture of Camp Tyson's second act after World War II ended.

INTRODUCTION

When I was little, I found a photograph in one of our family albums of a couple I did not know. It was one of those old dime store photo booth pictures of a young soldier and his wife. My mother told me they were the couple who had lived with the family during World War II. I realized that for the photograph to be included in our family album, the couple must have been important to us, and I wanted to know more.

From there, she and my grandmother and great-grandmother began telling me other stories about all the construction workers and their families who had lived in our house. Six families in all lived in our tiny house in Paris, Tennessee, during World War II, all at the same time.

Over time, I learned we were not the only family housing soldiers and construction workers and making sacrifices for Camp Tyson, which was located just outside of Paris and was the only barrage balloon training facility in the United States during the war. Most every family in Paris and nearby towns did the same. We used to take family drives through the former Camp Tyson, which by then was owned by a private company, and drive the since-abandoned old streets of the camp, where they would point out to me where the barracks had been, where the post exchange (PX) had been, and where the guard booths had been at the entrances.

As I grew into adulthood, I began learning that Camp Tyson was unique. Because it was the country's only barrage balloon training facility, its soldiers had an experience different from any other soldiers stationed anywhere during the war, and likewise, the experience of the people of Henry County, Tennessee, was unlike any other in the United States.

It was an everyday occurrence for Henry Countians to see the giant barrage balloons flying over Camp Tyson. They could be seen from just about anywhere in the county, all day, every day. But more importantly, Camp Tyson was a much-needed boon for the local economy. Most every household in the county was impacted by the US Army's decision to locate the camp in Henry County at a time when it was needed the most—right after the Great Depression.

Over time, the camp grew to 400 buildings and was home to 25,000 soldiers. It included 10 miles of asphalt roads, five miles of railroad, a hospital, a movie theater, a post office, a laundry, two chapels, a service club, several PX facilities, a library, sewer and electrical systems, motor pools, offices, a hydrogen generating plant, and its own water supply system. Some 3,000 German and Italian prisoners of war were quartered there as the war was coming to an end.

Camp Tyson also was home to the 320th Anti-Aircraft Barrage Balloon Battalion, the only all-black unit to land on the Normandy beaches on D-Day. Their contributions to the war effort were sadly largely overlooked, unknown not only to the people of Henry County at the time—both black and white—but also unheralded by the Army.

Henry County was selected for Camp Tyson in April 1941, and the camp was completed in March 1942. By February 13, 1942, the first balloon had been constructed at the camp and was set aloft by members of the 302nd Battalion.

As the war wound down, barrage balloons became obsolete. Camp Tyson was notified in April 1945 that it would be disbanded and its troops relocated.

A year after it closed, negotiations began behind the scenes, and the highest bidder for the property was the H.C. Spinks Clay Company. Thus began a whole new life for the old Camp Tyson, because its new owners, R.B. and Harriet Spinks Carothers, operated a cattle and horse ranch there in addition to the clay company. Generations of Henry Countians not only worked in unique positions for the company but also lived on the grounds, many in the old barracks that were fashioned into apartments.

The clay company continues today as the Lhoist Spinks Clay Company, with owners from Belgium, but remnants of Camp Tyson still remain: the old offices, motor pools, and the 90-foot-hangar in which the barrage balloons were constructed and which still is used by the company today.

One

FLYING ELEPHANTS

They were called "Flying Elephants" and "Gas Bags." And, because they were filled with hydrogen in combat and sometimes even in training, they were given the even more vivid name "Flying Bombs."

They were barrage balloons and they flew over Camp Tyson in Routon, Tennessee, on a daily basis during World War II. The residents of Henry County were in the unique position of being the only people in the United States who could look up at any time during the day and see the romantic and awe-inspiring sight of a sky full of these giant balloons.

Henry Countians, young and old, were fascinated by them.

Camp Tyson was the only barrage balloon training facility in the United States during World War II. The soldiers there not only learned how to fly the huge balloons, they also built them and were trained on a daily basis in how to construct, inflate, deflate, and utilize them in combat.

What that meant is that the soldiers at Camp Tyson shared a unique experience. Their activities, instruction, and routines were unlike any experienced by other servicemen during the war.

Largely overlooked in the history books, barrage balloons played an essential role in the war. Used by Camp Tyson–trained soldiers at D-Day and other key battles, the barrage balloons were both defensive and offensive weapons.

Of special significance in the Camp Tyson story is that it was home to the 320th Anti-Aircraft Barrage Balloon Battalion, the only all–African American unit to participate in the D-Day invasion.

From empty farm fields before the war, Camp Tyson would become a small city, with 400 buildings in all, miles of paved streets, more modern infrastructure than was available to the nearby towns at the time, and 25,000 soldiers. In the waning days of the war, some 3,000 German and Italian POWs were headquartered there.

Locating the camp in Henry County was a boon to the area, and as Camp Tyson grew, so did the city of Paris, becoming a boomtown overnight. Until now, Camp Tyson has lived on only in the collective—and fond—memories of the people of Henry County.

This is the story of Camp Tyson.

Camp Tyson was a small city—and a very modern one, especially compared to the closest nearby towns of Paris and McKenzie. Compared to the mostly rural area surrounding it, the camp was a modern marvel, with the US Army and federal government providing the modern infrastructure that Southern towns at that time lacked. This is Williams Street in Camp Tyson in a scene that shows how the living quarters were configured. (Author's collection.)

The soldiers' hard work began even before the camp was constructed. On the dusty country roads around Camp Tyson, platoons of soldiers with their motor vehicles and barrage balloons performed maneuvers daily, usually for hours at a time. This photograph was used for an Army press release issued on Sunday, May 2, 1943. The article released along with it apparently was intended to introduce the American public to Camp Tyson and its purpose. The camp had been in operation for a year but was unknown to most Americans. This photograph was taken at the intersection of Steele Road and Gate 3 Road, where Lou and Bettye Carter now live. The photograph is one of their prized possessions. (Courtesy of Lou and Bettye Carter.)

Two chapels were built for the camp, one on either side of the vast area, so that soldiers could be close to one wherever their barracks were located. This photograph shows one of the chapels under construction. According to the stamp on the back, this was taken at 11:45 a.m. on January 26, 1942, from a nearby roof in the southeast direction of Area No. 9. It is stamped "Barrage Balloon Training Center, Paris, Tennessee." It was taken by Paris photographer Frank Mason, who was hired by the Army to photograph the camp. (Courtesy of Wayne Webb.)

Both chapels were of good size and good construction and provided a choice of denominations for the soldiers. Chaplains were also available for counseling. The chapels were among the buildings that were bulldozed by the Army when the camp was closed after the war. Here is a photograph of one of the two chapels after its completion. (Courtesy of Wayne Webb.)

Construction of Camp Tyson was an arduous 24-hour-a-day operation that occurred over several weeks. Workers in the foreground are constructing a new building, and several barracks are already in place. The huge water tower that was part of the camp's modern infrastructure can be seen in the background. (Courtesy of Wayne Webb.)

The camp still looked pretty rough when it was under construction, but Army life had already begun in some areas while construction was ongoing in others. This photograph gives a view of the camp during the construction phase. (Courtesy of Wayne Webb.)

Former Camp Tyson soldiers held reunions years after the camp closed, and Wayne Webb of Mansfield, Tennessee, had the foresight to attend the reunions and make copies of photographs that belonged to those in attendance. For that reason, many photographs of the camp have been preserved, including this one of Camp Tyson construction underway at an unidentified building. Other parts of the camp are already active, with jeeps parked and people walking by. The photograph was taken by Frank Mason. (Courtesy of Wayne Webb.)

Rexie Smith of Routon was one of the workers who helped build the camp and in the process helped tear down some of the private properties that were claimed by eminent domain for the camp. His daughter, Nelda Pinson, now recalls those properties with sadness. "Daddy's first job out there was to assist in tearing down. I've found that the government can take, no matter how much you yank and pull." Smith also was a civilian employee at the Camp Tyson Fire Department. (Courtesy of Nelda Pinson.)

In the busy days while the camp was being built, there was a steady stream of both construction workers and their families and soldiers and their families moving into Henry County and the surrounding area. Families desperate for a job and a place to live would knock on doors in Paris, looking for any place they could find. Late one night, the Morris family on Walnut Street, in Paris, heard a knock on their door and found Lt. Col. Leon Moye on their doorstep. "We're going to spend the night with you tonight and then we're going to live with you," he said. Carol Morris Bowden said that despite her mother's protests, Colonel Moye was very persistent, and the officer and his wife lived with them for a year and became good friends. This picture of Moye was included in the 306th Coast Artillery yearbook from Camp Tyson. (Author's Collection.)

Construction of Camp Tyson provided good jobs for hundreds of workers who flocked to Paris from all over the region. Here, two men stop to pose with their equipment. The street has already been paved. Taken by Paris photographer Frank Mason, this is one of many items collected over the years by Wayne Webb. (Courtesy of Wayne Webb.)

Period cars dot the streets in this photograph taken by Frank Mason for the Army. Note the

already-completed barracks at left. (Courtesy of Wayne Webb.)

This is another view of the camp after it was completed. By the time this photograph was taken, the 90-foot barrage balloon hangar had been painted black. (Courtesy of Wayne Webb.)

The Paris photographer Frank Mason took this photograph of the water tower, and it is about as up close and personal as one can get. The checkerboard design on the top of the water tower was a sight that Henry Countians could see from miles around. The water tower was demolished around the 1980s, after the Camp Tyson grounds had been purchased by the Spinks Clay Company. The tower had deteriorated and was not used anymore when it was demolished. (Courtesy of Wayne Webb.)

APPRECIATION

Completion of Camp Tyson is a battle won for America!

Leadership in this phase of America's Defense was vital, but more important was the splendid and wholehearted co-operation with which the leaders were supplied.

As an order is carried out by a soldier, so was every instruction followed in earnest and with dispatch by the battalions of workers, both skilled and unskilled, white-collar and hand-workers, to give these United States its only Barrage Balloon Training Center.

A huge Army camp arose from what was once fields, pastures and woods.

Through the richness and fullness of its co-operation in this undertaking, Paris, Tennessee has displayed to the world that it is ready and willing to do its part in the fight for the preservation of the American Way of life.

And for all of which, the Rock City-Strider Construction Company is indeed truly grateful.

★

ROCK CITY-STRIDER CO.

PRIME CONTRACTORS

Once Camp Tyson was built, the main contractor, Rock City-Strider Company, paid for a fancy sepia-toned insert that was published in local newspapers. The insert contained several pages of copy and photographs welcoming Camp Tyson to the local area. The front page of the insert reads, "Completion of Camp Tyson is a battle won for America!" It notes, "A huge Army camp arose from what was once fields, pastures and woods. Through the richness and fullness of its cooperation in this undertaking, Paris, Tennessee, has displayed to the world that it is ready and willing to do its part in the fight for the preservation of the American way of life." (Author's collection.)

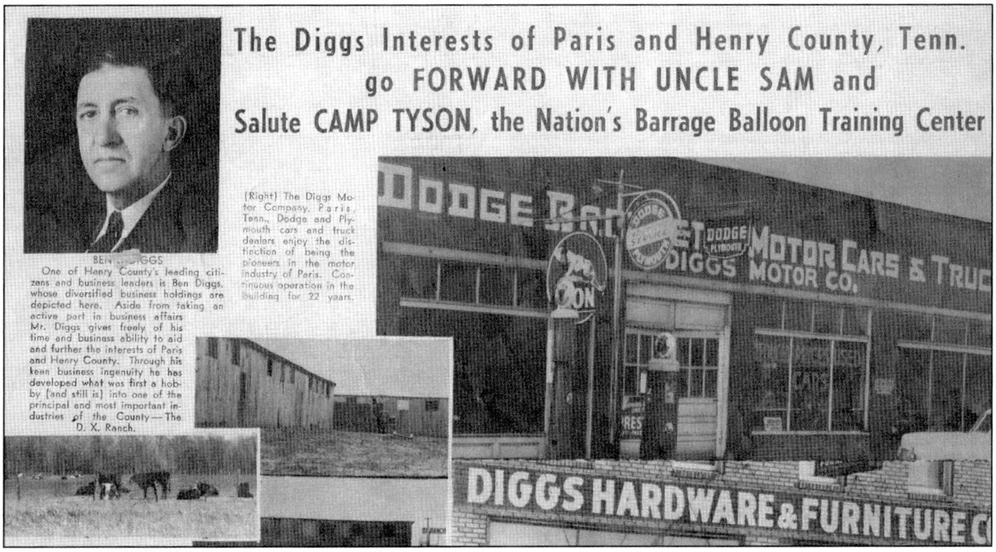

The Diggs Interests of Paris and Henry County, Tenn.
go FORWARD WITH UNCLE SAM and
Salute CAMP TYSON, the Nation's Barrage Balloon Training Center

BEN [illegible] DIGGS

One of Henry County's leading citizens and business leaders is Ben Diggs, whose diversified business holdings are depicted here. Aside from taking an active part in business affairs Mr. Diggs gives freely of his time and business ability to aid and further the interests of Paris and Henry County. Through his keen business ingenuity he has developed what was first a hobby (and still is) into one of the principal and most important industries of the County—The D. X. Ranch.

(Right) The Diggs Motor Company, Paris, Tenn., Dodge and Plymouth cars and truck dealers enjoy the distinction of being the pioneers in the motor industry of Paris. Continuous operation in the building for 22 years.

The newspaper insert welcoming Camp Tyson to the local area includes large advertisements from local companies, including this one from the Diggs Hardware and Furniture Company, one of the most prominent and long-standing businesses in Paris. (Author's collection.)

Blake Transport Co.

Mr. Blake, owner and operator of Blake Transport Company, operates a fleet of trucks between Paris and St. Louis, Missouri, serving West Tennessee and West Kentucky towns.

In connection with his transport business, he has added a Frozen Food Locker plant, which has made rapid growth and expects to expand into a 250 locker plant this Spring.

OUR WELCOME AND SALUTE TO CAMP TYSON, PARIS, TENN.

An advertisement from Blake's taxi service welcomes Camp Tyson to Paris. Owner Frank Blake, who later became mayor of Paris, later transformed his company into the bus service that transported soldiers and the public to and from the camp. (Author's collection.)

Huge crowds from all over the local area attended an open house for the public at Camp Tyson in 1942, called Army Day. Those attending were taken on tours of the camp and, of course, were encouraged to make a stop at the PX to buy souvenirs. Among those in attendance from the nearby town of McKenzie are, from left to right, Virginia Hudson, Carolyn Thompson, Martha and Margaret Adams, and Russellina and Kathleen Edwards. Carolyn Thompson later married Camp Tyson soldier Eddie Clericuzio, who stayed in McKenzie and operated the theater there for many years. (Courtesy of Joel Summers.)

Also at Army Day in 1942 were, from left to right, Margaret Adams, Russellene Hilliard (later Summers), R.B. Summers, and Martha Adams. (Courtesy of Joel Summers.)

The Army was in such a rush to open Camp Tyson to the public—and area residents were so anxious to see the camp—that construction was not yet totally complete for the first Army Day held at the camp in 1942. Visitors were using wooden walkways set up on dirt streets. (Courtesy of Joel Summers.)

The first balloon was set aloft on February 13, 1942, and an Army camera was there to capture the moment. The balloon was launched by members of the 302nd Battalion, and Howard Koenen of Murray, Kentucky, was one of the men who helped with the maneuver. Despite the fact that it was Friday the 13th, the first ascension was a success. Once the balloon was launched successfully, plans were immediately made for Camp Tyson's first visitor's day, which was held the next week. This photograph is from the 306th Coast Artillery Barrage Balloon yearbook. (Author's collection.)

Gen. John Maynard was the first commander of Camp Tyson and a commanding figure. He was born in 1887 in Virginia and had a storied career in the Army. He served in the Philippines and Hawaii during the war. Before assuming command of Camp Tyson in February 1942, he was in command of the Coast Artillery Replacement Training Center at Camp Wallace, Texas. While the camp was under construction, he lived in the mansion owned by the family of Sidney Mandle on Walnut Street in Paris (which is still there). Once his quarters were completed, he moved to the camp. After the camp closed and the grounds were purchased for the Spinks Clay Company, the general's quarters were converted into the home of the Carothers family, the clay company's owners. This photograph of General Maynard is featured on one of the first pages of the 306th Coast Artillery yearbook. (Author's collection.)

One of the items in demand at the Camp Tyson PX was the official booklet published by the Army. With a colorized cover and black-and-white photographs on the inside, the booklet described daily life for the soldiers. A few of the booklets still exist today and are prized possessions. (Author's collection.)

A postcard sold in the Camp Tyson PX depicts a large group of solders and supply trucks during maneuvers up and down the wooded and hilly countryside near the camp, along with very low altitude (VLA) barrage balloons. (Courtesy of Lou and Bettye Carter.)

Soldiers and their jeeps are kicking up a lot of dust on a lonely dirt road while performing maneuvers with a barrage balloon. This was a familiar sight to rural Henry Countians during the war. (Courtesy of Wayne Webb.)

Paris photographer Frank Mason took this photograph, which shows the expanse of the huge Camp Tyson grounds. The US government purchased 2,000 acres for the camp in August 1941, and some 8,000 men were involved in building the camp. (Courtesy of Wayne Webb.)

The Army was very involved in publicizing Camp Tyson, and camera crews from *Stars and Stripes* and other military publications were on the grounds on a regular basis, taking photographs and sending out press releases to the Associated Press and United Press International for use in newspapers and magazines. Here is an Army camera crew on March 9, 1943. (Courtesy of Tennessee State Library and Archives.)

These men represented an integral part of the Camp Tyson story. The faculty and staff worked hard to train the men in the use and operation of barrage balloons. (Courtesy of Wayne Webb.)

This view of the camp shows the barracks flowing down curved streets. Camp Tyson was kept in tip-top shape at all times, as was required at any Army camp. (Courtesy of Wayne Webb.)

Two

Why Henry County?

Locating the United States' only barrage balloon training facility in rural Henry County, Tennessee, was no accident. Henry County was in an especially remote area in the 1940s, far from both coasts, which were considered prime targets for the country's enemies. It was rural, isolated, and still suffering the effects of the Depression.

The Army had begun experimenting with barrage balloons as a defensive measure even before Pearl Harbor was attacked in 1941. A temporary facility was established at Camp Davis, North Carolina, with some training conducted there, and the Army began seeking a permanent barrage balloon training facility.

The tiny community of Routon, Tennessee, was selected in April 1941. Its isolation was perfect for the Army: Henry County was out of the way of regular air traffic and was largely out of the public eye, which meant it also was out of the eye of the enemy. The county is located on a plentiful water supply, and importantly, it also boasted natural and reliable wind currents that were necessary for training.

Locating Camp Tyson in Henry County was an immediate boon to the area. The people of the county received the news that the government would purchase 2,000 acres of land to build the camp on August 15, 1941.

Local newspapers described how almost immediately traffic on the roads into Paris was bumper-to-bumper, with hundreds of men and their families streaming into Paris and the surrounding towns looking for construction jobs and places to live.

The city of Paris opened its arms to them, providing housing in every available nook and cranny, from sheds to back porches.

Soon, most every home in Paris and the county was crowded—and many were just plain overcrowded—with several families living under the same roof.

History was being made at Camp Tyson and as it grew, so did Paris. The camp impacted the city greatly, transforming it from a small town to a city.

Overnight, Paris became a boomtown.

Chances are that any time a soldier's family came to visit him in Paris, they would stay at Hotel Greystone. The fanciest hotel for miles around, its visitors included the famous Rothschild family. Howard Rothschild used to play the piano in the Greystone's lobby on his free evenings away from the camp. The Greystone was known to be a good place for local girls, who worked as waitresses, to meet soldiers. Nell McBride of Paris remembered that it was a bustling spot. "Were there ever a lot of soldiers there?" she said. "Oh me. It was quite a lively place." The Greystone is still in operation at the corner of Washington and Fentress Streets in Paris. (Both, author's collection.)

One of the busiest spots in all of Henry County was the Camp Tyson bus station, located at the corner of Brewer and Wood Streets in Paris. Before the camp opened, there was no public transportation in Paris, but with hundreds of people coming to town, it became a real need. One of the first to see the need and act on it was Frank Blake. He applied for and received a government contract to establish a bus line from Camp Tyson to Paris, a distance of seven miles. He converted his tire store into the bus depot. The buses operated 24 hours a day, with round trips on a 30-minute schedule for both citizens and soldiers. (Author's collection.)

One of the ways that Camp Tyson became part of the local communities was by holding parades showcasing the soldiers and their smaller barrage balloons. Here, children run after a barrage balloon being displayed in a parade on South Poplar Street around the court square in downtown Paris. The Commercial Bank Building is at left. Huge crowds lined the streets for the parade, which included soldiers, vehicles, and balloons from Camp Tyson. (Courtesy of Virgil Wall.)

The parade—with the camp band blaring—marches down a residential street in the nearby town of McKenzie on the way to the town square. (Courtesy of Wayne Webb.)

A boy on a bicycle rides in front of the parade as it rounds the court square on Poplar Street in Paris. One of the small barrage balloons is fastened to a jeep, and African American soldiers keep hold of it with ropes. (Courtesy of Wayne Webb.)

People in Paris were excited about the parade passing by. Note the crowd standing on the roof of the Irvin Lee store on the right and the ladies watching the parade from the second-floor windows above Murray Jewelers. (Courtesy of Wayne Webb.)

Another view of the parade through downtown Paris shows the Camp Tyson band in full swing. The band was a good one and big, complete with tubas, a large horn section, and a drum major leading the band. (Courtesy of Wayne Webb.)

Camp Tyson had two PX facilities on base, and both were happening places, selling sundry items for the soldiers and officers who lived on the base but also offering souvenir items for the public. Many local households still have Camp Tyson items that were sold there, from fancy silk pillowcases to postcards. Here is a photograph of a Camp Tyson PX during an especially busy time at Christmas. (Courtesy of Rebecca Goins.)

Three

Paris Opens Its Doors

It is no exaggeration to say that most everyone in Henry County owed their livelihood to Camp Tyson. Rural West Tennessee was still reeling from the Depression. Camp Tyson produced much needed jobs, both at the camp itself and through the side businesses that developed.

Quick-minded local entrepreneurs of all ages produced their own enterprises, from providing bus services to opening restaurants to providing hundreds of daily sack lunches for troop trains. Even enterprising youngsters got into it, making money selling Coca-Colas and shining shoes.

Old timers in Paris credit the camp with making the town a much richer place culturally through the influence of the soldiers, especially those who settled there after the war, marrying local women and bringing their unique heritage and cultures to the area.

It is a testament to the impact that Camp Tyson had that so many people have vivid memories of their days working there and hosting families even though much time has passed. Most every household has kept some remembrance of the camp, whether it be postcards, phone books, or pillowcases.

A real bond developed because of Camp Tyson that endures. Many local people are still in touch with the former soldiers and families who stayed with them over 60 years ago. "They became like family" is the refrain heard over and over again.

Jeanne Anderson Townsend of Paris, who worked as a secretary for officers at the camp, said that other Southern towns were not as welcoming to the Army camps as Paris. Some did not want that many Yankees coming to their towns, she said. "Other cities did not absorb them like we did. It made for a very comfortable existence for everyone here during the war."

It was a difficult time, definitely, but also an exciting time. Spurred by the anxiety of war, it was a time for sacrifice, hard work, fast changes, fast friendships, high-flying balloons, and romance.

J.J. Olive has fond memories of the Camp Tyson days and the soldiers who enjoyed the hospitality at his family's farm in rural Henry County. His parents, Eldon and Humie Olive, opened their home to the soldiers, especially for Sunday dinners with good country cooking. His aunt and uncle, Jessie and Minnie Olive, are pictured here with three soldiers from the camp during one such occasion. (Courtesy of J.J. Olive.)

The home of Eldon and Humie Olive, near the tiny town of Como, was a gathering place for Camp Tyson soldiers, many of whom kept in touch with them after the war. Humie was a good cook, and Sunday dinners were always open to soldiers at the camp, according to their son J.J. Olive. A group of soldiers and local girls are pictured here at the Olive home. (Courtesy of J.J. Olive.)

Among many soldiers who were married in one of the Camp Tyson chapels was 2nd Lt. George Francis Batchelder of Lisbon Falls, Maine, who was married to his sweetheart, Mary Anastasia Sylvester of Portland, Maine, on September 5, 1942, by Catholic chaplain Captain Rivers. Their daughter Ann Batchelder Gorman said the ceremony included a 5:00 p.m. Mass with music by the camp organist. The wedding dinner was held at the Greystone Hotel in Paris, and the couple honeymooned at the Peabody in Memphis. While Batchelder was stationed at the camp, his wife stayed in the Barton Apartments in Paris. (Courtesy of Ann Batchelder Gorman.)

Wayne King had many memories revolving around Camp Tyson. His father, Bob King, was a military policeman in the Army and told the officers at Camp Tyson that the family owned Shady Park Trailer Camp, where soldiers would be welcome. On weekends, hundreds of Camp Tyson soldiers enjoyed the dance hall and restaurant at Shady Park. (Courtesy of Wayne King.)

Cal Orris was one of many Camp Tyson soldiers who married local girls and stayed in the area after World War II. Cal saw Maxine Etheridge walking down the street in Paris and told the soldiers he was with that he was going to marry her. "I don't know who she is, but I'm going to find out," he said. He called her that night and told her they would be married someday. Maxine told him he was crazy, and he said, "I may be crazy, but I'm nice crazy and I'm going to keep calling you until you agree to go out with me." (Courtesy of Susan Orris Palmer.)

Cal Orris had his photograph taken in his Army uniform by Paris photographer Frank Mason, who took many photographs for Camp Tyson and also catered to the soldiers for their individual professional photographs. (Courtesy of Susan Orris Palmer.)

As a soldier, John Little received quartermaster training at Camp Tyson, after which he was sent to Europe, was part of the D-Day invasion, and was captured in June 1944 in Normandy. During the capture, he was shot in the leg by German soldiers. He was taken to a Berlin hospital and then moved from prison camp to prison camp. He was finally freed in 1945. While at Camp Tyson, he and his wife, Helen, lived in the basement at Pearl Routon's home on Dunlap Street in Paris. (Courtesy of Tom Little.)

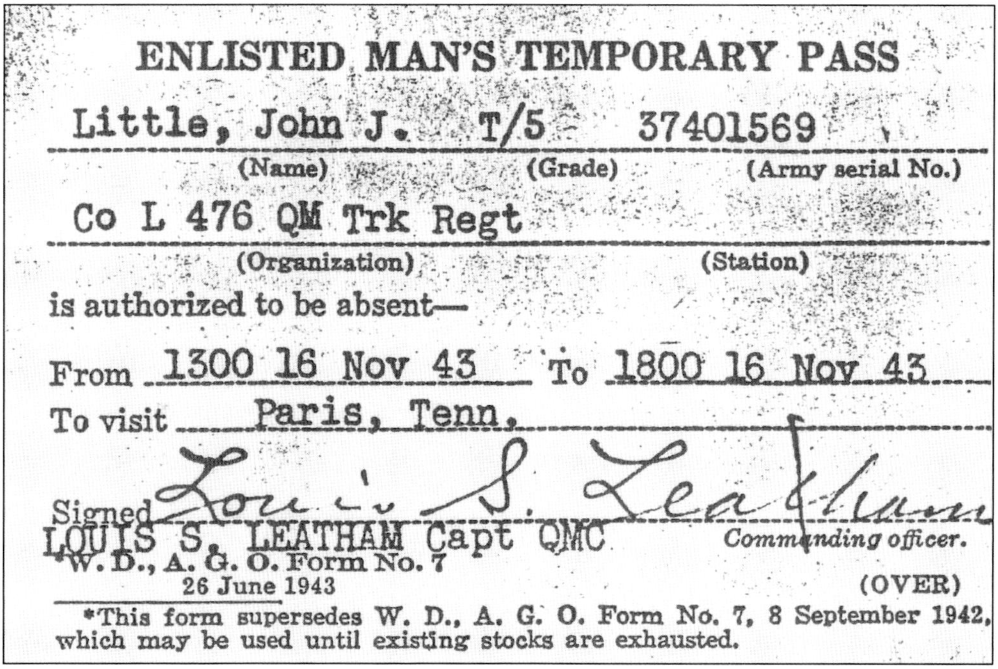

ENLISTED MAN'S TEMPORARY PASS

Little, John J. T/5 37401569
(Name) (Grade) (Army serial No.)

Co L 476 QM Trk Regt
(Organization) (Station)

is authorized to be absent—

From 1300 16 Nov 43 To 1800 16 Nov 43

To visit Paris, Tenn.

Signed Louis S. Leatham
LOUIS S. LEATHAM Capt QMC Commanding officer.

*W. D., A. G. O. Form No. 7
26 June 1943 (OVER)

*This form supersedes W. D., A. G. O. Form No. 7, 8 September 1942, which may be used until existing stocks are exhausted.

Among the memorabilia that John Little saved from Camp Tyson is this pass he was granted to travel from the camp into Paris. (Courtesy of Tom Little.)

More memorabilia that John Little saved includes a ticket to the service club. An evening of entertainment and relaxation at the club cost 25¢. (Courtesy of Tom Little.)

One of the sweetest love stories is that of Loyal Whiteside and Sue Edwards Wagner. The two met while he was a soldier at Camp Tyson, and a romance was sparked. But Whiteside married his hometown sweetheart in Pennsylvania, and Wagner married another Camp Tyson soldier named Hugh Wagner from Wisconsin. Many years later, after their spouses had passed, their romance was rekindled and they talked of marriage. But it was not to be. Sadly, Wagner died before they could take that step. Whiteside said, "We were happy to have found each other and happy at how things were." (Courtesy of Loyal Whiteside.)

Four

The Workforce

When the people of Henry County learned that the US government was locating a barrage balloon facility near Routon, no one yet knew what a barrage balloon was. Neither did they know that it would be the only one of its kind in the United States. And frankly, they didn't care. All they knew was that the announcement meant there would be lots of jobs with the opening of the camp.

After the announcement, the contracts were let quickly, with the Rock City–Strider Construction Company of Nashville being the construction manager. The remainder of the jobs were subcontracted to area and local contractors, providing a needed boost to the local economy.

Local newspapers reported on the truck- and trainloads of building materials that were flowing into the site and the hundreds of workmen who were pouring into the area.

The workmen were building a modern military camp from what just weeks before were acres of farm fields. The work was performed 24 hours a day, and progress was rapid.

Charlie McClure of Paris worked for decades for the Spinks Clay Company, which purchased the property after the camp closed following the war. He took it upon himself to preserve the history of Camp Tyson and wrote a history of all he remembered.

According to McClure, the initial phase of the camp occupied 1,680 acres, with a second phase following that with even more acreage. Over time, the camp developed into a modern facility with 10 miles of asphalt roads, 400 buildings, five miles of railroad, a post office, two chapels, a hospital, a service club, a library, a theater, guest housing, a hydrogen generating plant, state-of-the-art electrical and sewer supply systems, motor pools, numerous offices, several PX facilities, an industrial-sized laundry, and its own water supply system that was symbolized by the huge water tower that used to stand sentry over the grounds.

And then there was the 90-foot-tall hangar, which still is on the grounds. During the war, the hangar was used to construct the barrage balloons. After the war, it was used to sort clay for the Spinks Clay Company. Today, it still is used by its new owners, the Lhoist Spinks Clay Company of Belgium.

Jerry Ridgeway's mother, Edith Moser Ridgeway of Paris, was one of hundreds of young ladies who worked as civilian employees at the camp. According to Jerry, her mother worked for the camp commander, Gen. John Maynard. She posed for this photograph with a few soldiers and construction workers. The photograph was taken while the camp was still being built and is labelled "Edith and friends." (Courtesy of Jerry Ridgeway.)

Two female civilian employees walk through the streets of the camp, presumably back to their offices. Camp Tyson employed many women from the local area in a wide variety of positions in the offices. (Courtesy of Wayne Webb.)

Camp Tyson had plenty of manpower for all the jobs that were required for the operation of a military installation, but it was also dependent on local civilians. Doris McCutchen of Paris, at right, was one of the many local ladies who worked at the camp. She is pictured assisting 1st Lt. Albert Leach and Maj. J.B. Mankin in the staff offices. This photograph was included in the 306th Coast Artillery yearbook. (Author's collection.)

Pictured in front of the administration building is a group of female civilian employees with a female officer, whose names are listed on the back of this 1941 photograph: Mrs. Dreiss, Reggie Roney, Juanita Fitch, Ethel Dinkins, Red ?, Pauline Greer, Miss Henry, Lieutenant Opgrand, Onida Osborn, Mrs. Rowe, Pasalee McAdoo, and Sue Platt. (Courtesy of Wayne Webb.)

Once the camp was up and running, most everyone in Henry County (and much of the surrounding area) was dependent on it for their livelihoods. A Miss Paschall from Henry County is shown helping Sergeant Warren and 1st Lt. Leonard Adler at one of the camp offices. (Author's collection.)

Civilian employees Edith Paschall (left) and Mary Jo Burke pose in front of the 3rd Echelon motor repair shop office. Jeanne Townsend of Paris still has several photographs of the ladies who worked with her in the camp offices, as well as warm memories of her time working at Camp Tyson. (Courtesy of Jeanne Townsend.)

Several civilian employees pose in front of an office building where they worked at the camp. Camp Tyson not only provided a good living for local women but also provided them a way to ease their anxieties about the war by getting involved in the war effort. For many Henry County women, it was the first time they were called upon to provide for their families. The jobs provided valuable work experience that they put to use after the war. (Courtesy of Rebecca Goins.)

John Steele was hired by the federal government to mow the huge grounds of Camp Tyson, using four teams of mules. His grandson Joe Lankford said he was paid $1 an hour for the job, and the family still has Steele's invoices. Ironically, the Steele family was among those whose land was taken by eminent domain for the camp. John Steele is pictured here with one of his teams. (Courtesy of Joe Lankford.)

An unidentified woman, presumably a civilian employee of the Signal Corps office, poses with one of the corps' cars at the camp. (Courtesy of Wayne Webb.)

Pearl Routon played an important role in the history of Camp Tyson—many roles, actually. As proprietor of a restaurant in the tiny town of Routon, where Camp Tyson was located, she also operated a group of cabins and was postmistress. She also had a green thumb and was known for her beautiful gardens. Here, she is smiling widely on her tractor in the fields of Routon as barrage balloons float overhead. (Courtesy of Jill Routon Wilson.)

A group of telephone operators stands in front of a car on one of the streets at the camp. Note the chapel in the left background. (Courtesy of Wayne Webb.)

Five

A Soldier's Life

The use of barrage balloons was begun in Europe during World War I by the Allied powers. The United States began using them during World War II, when they were developed first by the Army Air Corps and then placed in service by the Coast Artillery and Marine Corps.

Barrage balloons were used to deter invasion by low-flying aircraft. As they were filled with hydrogen, they would explode when enemy aircraft flew through their unseen cables. They were also used to shield Allied positions, which could not be seen because of the barrage balloons, forcing enemy planes to fly at higher altitudes.

The Barrage Balloon Training Center included five battalions by the fall of 1941, with the first balloon being launched at Camp Tyson on February 13, 1942, by the 302nd Barrage Balloon Battalion. Howard Koenen of Murray, Kentucky, was one of the men in that battalion and remembered that day well. "It was quite an accomplishment and we had a big celebration that day." By the end of the war, there were 17 units stationed there.

Training for the soldiers consisted of daily maneuvers, camping out, and running up and down the hills of Henry County with the barrage balloons launched from Army jeeps. It also included field training off-base, such as from barges and the bridge at Kentucky Lake at what is now Paris Landing State Park.

Balloon beds were constructed at the camp consisting of concrete circles with tie-downs to anchor the balloons to the ground so that they could be inflated and deflated during training.

Most of the balloon beds and tie-downs were bulldozed by farmers after the war, but several have been preserved, notably on the farms of John Steele and Joe Lankford. The only complete balloon bed still preserved is on Lankford's farm on Steele Road.

These military policemen were photographed for the 306th Coast Artillery yearbook reviewing paperwork at the camp. As they did at other Army camps, MPs had the unenviable duty of policing and patrolling the camp, often having to discipline their fellow soldiers. (Author's collection.)

A couple of rather formidable-looking MPs pause for a photograph in front of their offices. Camp Tyson had its share of rowdy soldiers who were required to spend time in the stockade every now and then. A "detachment" is a military unit smaller than the battalion to which it is attached. (Courtesy of Wayne Webb.)

Former soldier Loyal Whiteside, who now lives in Florida, has boxes full of mementoes he kept from his Camp Tyson days. Among the items are a detailed scrapbook with photographs of himself and his buddies at camp and during visits to Paris. He also kept this large photograph of the 317th Battalion, Company B, of which he was a member. (Courtesy of Loyal Whiteside.)

Among the items in Loyal Whiteside's scrapbook of Camp Tyson mementoes is this postcard. The rendering depicts a Camp Tyson jeep and soldier in an action pose that probably was never used in real life. Postcards like this one were sold at the Camp Tyson PX. (Courtesy of Loyal Whiteside.)

The US Signal Corps released this photograph of evening retreat at Camp Tyson for publicity purposes. Former soldiers at Camp Tyson described evening retreat as a welcome sound throughout the camp, because they knew they could finally relax for a little while. (Courtesy of the family of Eddie Moody.)

Soldiers stand at attention along the rolling hills of the camp. In the right background is an area reserved for target practice. This photograph is one of several donated to the Paris–Henry County Heritage Center by Leander A. Larsen. Larsen was a private first class at the camp during the war. He married a local girl, Rose Veltman of Paris. Larsen was born in Norway in 1906 and died in Brooklyn, New York, in November 1992. (Courtesy of the Paris–Henry County Heritage Center.)

Camp Tyson was outfitted with a variety of specialized equipment used in training soldiers to maneuver and utilize the huge barrage balloons. This photograph shows a type of winch that was used to raise and lower barrage balloons in 1943. Leander A. Larsen donated this photograph to the Paris–Henry County Heritage Center. (Courtesy of the Paris–Henry County Heritage Center.)

Soldiers gather for morning call, which was conducted at sunrise to wake the camp's sleepy soldiers. In this photograph, members of the medical detachment pose in front of their headquarters. (Courtesy of James Wilson.)

The equipment used at Camp Tyson was rugged and made to last. Former soldier Leander Larson donated this photograph to the Paris–Henry County Heritage Center with the notation that it was taken in 1943. Larson did not identify the piece of equipment. (Courtesy of the Paris–Henry County Heritage Center.)

Col. W.H. Dunham instructs a soldier in the proper way to operate the all-important piece of equipment, the winch. Colonel Dunham succeeded General Maynard as commander of the camp. Colonel Dunham originally served as chief of the barrage balloon division, and this photograph was taken while he was overseeing the barrage balloon units. The caption to this photograph in Herston Cooper's self-published pamphlet, *Remembering Camp Tyson*, reads "Wrench? No. Wench? Oh, no. WINCH? YES!" (Courtesy of Wayne Webb.)

Much hard and exacting work was performed inside the huge 90-foot hangar, which was used to construct the barrage balloons. Pictured is a Mark VI portable LA BB winch, which was used to raise and lower the barrage balloons. This photograph was donated to the Paris–Henry County Heritage Center by Leander Larsen. (Courtesy of the Paris–Henry County Heritage Center.)

Soldiers are hard at work doing what was surely one of their least favorite activities: cleaning the barracks. Former Camp Tyson soldiers said the barracks were kept clean because they never knew when an inspection might happen. This photograph was donated to the Paris–Henry County Heritage Center by Leander Larsen. (Courtesy of the Paris–Henry County Heritage Center.)

James Wilson of Paris was a sergeant assigned to the medical company at the camp. Wilson and his buddy Cedric Knott are pictured in front of a barrage balloon with several other soldiers in one of the most iconic photographs taken at Camp Tyson. Members of the Army camera crew were impressed with Wilson's rugged good looks and asked him to be a model for photographs used with press releases. Knott is third from left, and Wilson is third from right. (Courtesy of James Wilson.)

Tall and short human MPs pose with their big and small canine MPs at the camp. The sight of these four must have drawn laughs from the other soldiers. (Courtesy of Wayne Webb.)

James Wilson (third from left) poses with members of the medical and dental detachment at the entrance of the medical company during a visit by Army photographers. (Courtesy of James Wilson.)

Camp Tyson soldiers pass in review in front of officers during inspection exercises. Inspection was a regular occurrence in the busy days of Camp Tyson soldiers. Among the soldiers are James Wilson (first row, far left) and Cedric Knott (second row, far left), both of Paris. (Author's collection.)

James Wilson posed for his formal portrait in uniform. Like many portraits of the day, it was a black-and-white photograph that was colorized by the photographer. (Courtesy of James Wilson.)

One of the more exacting jobs at Camp Tyson was operating the winches that controlled the barrage balloons. Like the barrage balloons, winches came in various sizes; some were built to be mounted on jeeps, while others were smaller, more mobile, and could be moved over ground. (Author's collection.)

Soldiers, including James Wilson of Paris, at right, pose in one of the Army vehicles at the camp. The vehicle sports two license plates: one for the state of Tennessee and the other to identify it as being from Camp Tyson. (Courtesy of James Wilson.)

In this photograph included in the 306th Coast Artillery yearbook, soldiers at Camp Tyson stand at attention after successfully inflating a barrage balloon during training exercises. (Author's collection.)

Lt. Col. Donald Sensing works at his desk at Camp Tyson in this photograph from the 306th Coast Artillery yearbook. (Author's collection.)

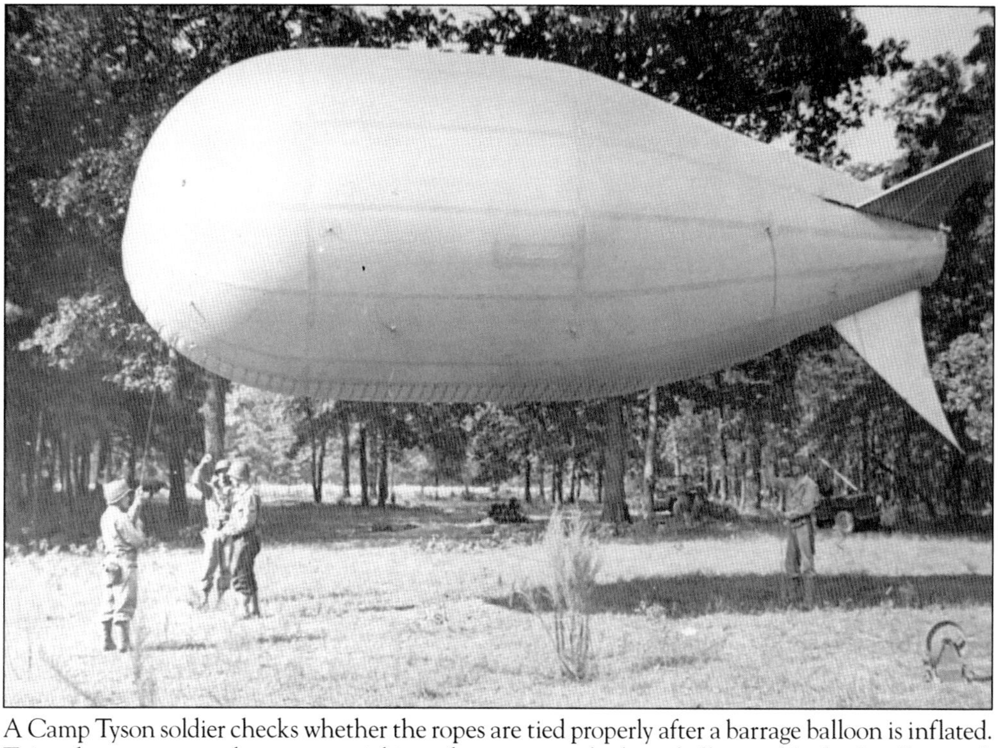

A Camp Tyson soldier checks whether the ropes are tied properly after a barrage balloon is inflated. Tying the ropes properly was essential in order to secure the huge balloons. (Author's collection.)

By design, Camp Tyson was out of the way of both coasts, but that did not mean it left its guard down. The men and women of Camp Tyson took the same steps to protect themselves and their camp as did others anywhere in the United States. This is one of several ammunition bunkers on the grounds at Camp Tyson. The bunkers can still be found on the grounds. (Courtesy of Wayne Webb.)

Camp Tyson commander Gen. John Maynard, left, took time out for a bit of bass fishing on nearby Kentucky Lake with former Paris mayor J.P. Lasater. Lasater was mayor during the Camp Tyson years and worked hard to ensure that the citizens of Paris opened their doors to the soldiers and construction workers who flocked into the city when the camp opened. (Courtesy of Stephanie Taylor.)

Loyal Whiteside is shown in his dress uniform. He has kept many scrapbooks from his Camp Tyson days. Whiteside lives in Florida now and said he has fond memories of his time at Camp Tyson. (Courtesy of Loyal Whiteside.)

Probably some of the busiest and hottest jobs at Camp Tyson were those in the bakery. That probably accounts for the serious faces on these men. (Courtesy of Wayne Webb.)

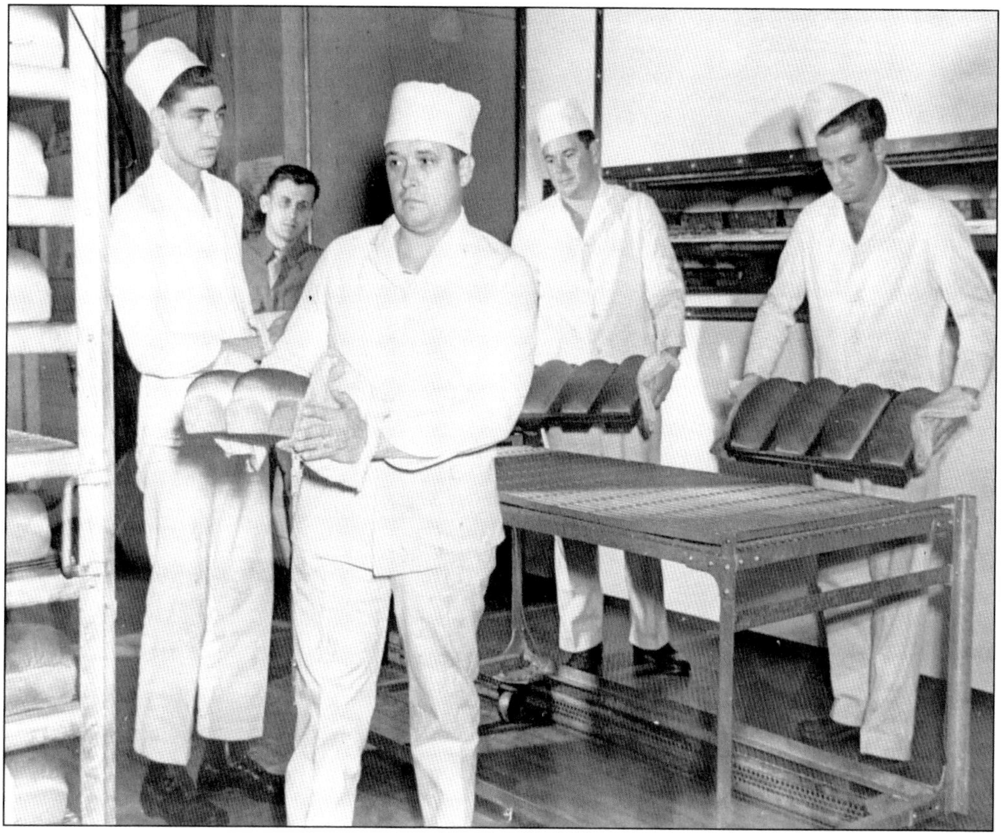

When working with huge barrage balloons, it was essential that soldiers knew how to properly tie knots. In this photograph, which was included in the Coast Artillery yearbook, soldiers are shown learning the ropes of knot-tying. (Author's collection.)

This was the mess hall for the military police, with a sign declaring "This Mess is Rated the Best Mess in Camp Tyson for the Past Month." Note that both black and white MPs are pictured. (Courtesy of Wayne Webb.)

In this photograph taken by the US Signal Corps, the caption states that these Women's Army Corps (WAC) officers had arrived on a two-hour-late coal burner (or train) and apparently arrived very hungry. The notation on the back says, "WAC officers eating first meal at Camp Tyson 1943." Note the flowers on their table. (Courtesy of Wayne Webb.)

In a photograph used for the camp newspaper the *Gas Bag*, an unidentified female civilian employee and officer check over papers. The photograph is stamped as having been taken by the US Signal Corps. (Courtesy of Wayne Webb.)

Four soldiers train with a medium-sized barrage balloon in a field on the camp. Note the tie-down in the right foreground holding the balloon in place. Most of these tie-downs have been removed by farmers who purchased the land after the camp closed. However, a few remain. (Courtesy of Wayne Webb.)

In this photograph, included in the 306th Coast Artillery yearbook, soldiers learn how to work with the barrage balloons, using a small model. Soldiers were better able to understand the intricacies of the barrage balloons when working with miniatures. (Author's collection.)

These military policemen on their motorcycles are ready to roar into action. In a camp the size of Camp Tyson, motorcycles were a good way for the MPs to get around. (Courtesy of Wayne Webb.)

Displaying the attitude prevalent during World War II of not wasting anything, an officer points to a sign near the garbage bins outside a mess hall. The photograph is stamped "Public Relations Officer, Camp Tyson, Tennessee" on the back. (Courtesy of Wayne Webb.)

Captain Overton works from his desk in this undated photograph taken by the US Signal Corps. Overton was the finance officer at Camp Tyson. He is shown exchanging papers with an unidentified officer. (Courtesy of Wayne Webb.)

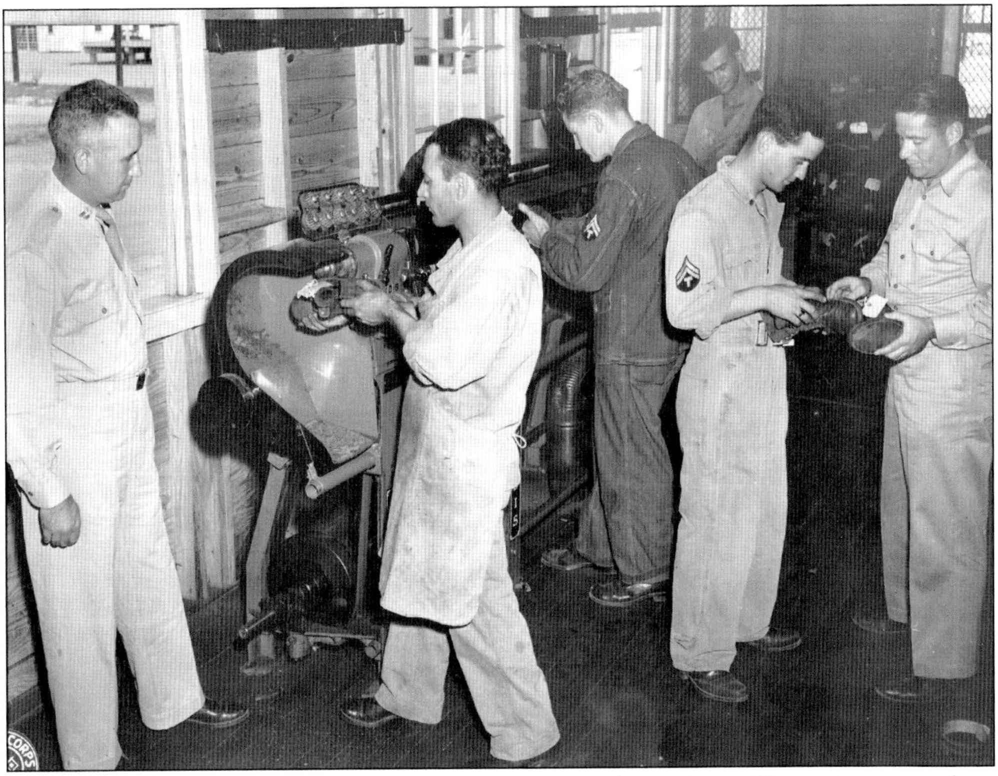

Appearing spiffy was important for soldiers and officers at the camp. Soldiers are seen here repairing shoes. The photograph was taken by the US Army Signal Corps. (Courtesy of Wayne Webb.)

Capt. Herb Adams poses near the barracks. He was one of the camp's military policemen. Notice how tidy the camp was, with small picket fences around the yards. Some street signs can be seen. (Courtesy of Wayne Webb.)

Col. W.H. Dunham Jr. was the commander of the barrage balloon training center from 1943 to 1944, which was just a portion of his distinguished military career. He also succeeded Gen. John Maynard as camp commander. While assigned to the Coast Artillery Corps, he served in the Philippines, Hawaii, and Panama in World Wars I and II. During World War II, he served as chief of the barrage balloon division of the anti-aircraft command in Richmond before being assigned to Camp Tyson. In this photograph, Dunham is at left. The US Army Signal Corps stamp on the back of the photograph indicates that it was taken in 1943. The couple in the photograph are not identified. (Courtesy of Wayne Webb.)

Target practice was employed on a regular basis, and to keep things interesting—and provide a lot of motivation—Camp Tyson used unique targets. These homemade targets depicting the heads of Mussolini, Hitler, and Tojo were used for target practice and were acquired in 2015 by the Henry County Historical Society at an estate sale for James and Emily Cox. The heads had been acquired years before by the Cox family after the camp closed. They are now on display at the Paris–Henry County Heritage Center. (Author's collection).

The Camp Tyson stockade was for soldiers who committed infractions of various sorts. The stockade was later used for German POWs. (Courtesy of Wayne Webb.)

Prisoners were given their daily exercise but used wooden guns weighted with lead. Note how threadbare their clothing is, with some of the prisoners not even buttoning up their shirts. (Courtesy of Wayne Webb.)

Chaplain Peter Vroom looks earnest as he speaks to a visitor in his office at Camp Tyson. As at any Army camp, chaplains at Camp Tyson were kept busy as soldiers from all over the country tried to adjust not only to Army life but also to being far away from home. Reverend Vroom was raised in Paterson, New Jersey, and served as an Army chaplain from 1941 to 1945. After the war, he served at several Baptist churches in Indiana, Pennsylvania, and West Virginia. (Courtesy of Wayne Webb.)

This undated photograph provides a wide view of some of the Camp Tyson offices. It also supplies a rare view of the rail spur that was built into the camp from the lines that ran through the nearby towns of Paris and McKenzie. Note that the huge water tower in the background has not yet been painted in its iconic checkerboard pattern that Henry Countians remember. (Courtesy of Wayne Webb.)

The caption for this image in the 306th Coast Artillery yearbook says this is "The 306th in Action," although they don't look all that energetic. The 306th Coast Artillery Barrage Balloon Battalion was one of the units assigned to Camp Tyson. The 306th was activated at Camp Tyson in February 1942 and was under the supervision of Lt. Col. J.H. Gilbert. (Author's collection.)

A balloon flies over the barracks with helium canisters placed nearby for training. A ready and plentiful supply of helium was essential for a camp that specialized in the operation of barrage balloons. (Courtesy of Charlie Allen.)

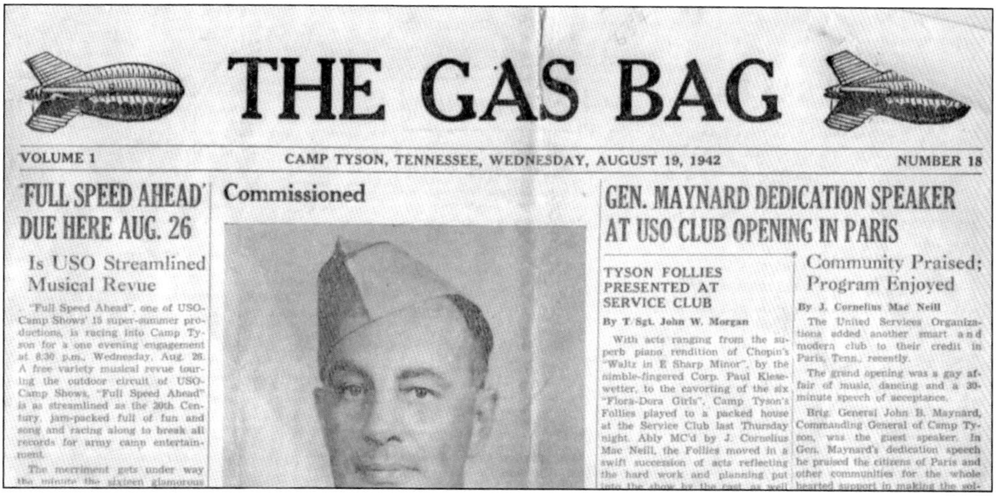

THE GAS BAG

VOLUME 1 — CAMP TYSON, TENNESSEE, WEDNESDAY, AUGUST 19, 1942 — NUMBER 18

'FULL SPEED AHEAD' DUE HERE AUG. 26

Is USO Streamlined Musical Revue

"Full Speed Ahead", one of USO-Camp Shows' 15 super-summer productions, is racing into Camp Tyson for a one evening engagement at 8:30 p.m., Wednesday, Aug. 26. A free variety musical revue touring the outdoor circuit of USO-Camp Shows, "Full Speed Ahead" is as streamlined as the 20th Century, jam-packed full of fun and song and racing along to break all records for army camp entertainment.

The merriment gets under way

Commissioned

GEN. MAYNARD DEDICATION SPEAKER AT USO CLUB OPENING IN PARIS

TYSON FOLLIES PRESENTED AT SERVICE CLUB

By T/Sgt. John W. Morgan

With acts ranging from the superb piano rendition of Chopin's "Waltz in E Sharp Minor", by the nimble-fingered Corp. Paul Kiesewetter, to the cavorting of the six "Flora-Dora Girls", Camp Tyson's Follies played to a packed house at the Service Club last Thursday night. Ably MC'd by J. Cornelius Mac Neill, the Follies moved in a swift succession of acts reflecting the hard work and planning put

Community Praised; Program Enjoyed

By J. Cornelius Mac Neill

The United Services Organizations added another smart and modern club to their credit in Paris, Tenn., recently.

The grand opening was a gay affair of music, dancing and a 30-minute speech of acceptance.

Brig. General John B. Maynard, Commanding General of Camp Tyson, was the guest speaker. In Gen. Maynard's dedication speech he praised the citizens of Paris and other communities for the whole

The Camp Tyson newspaper was called the *Gas Bag*, a fitting name since that was one of the nicknames the soldiers gave to the barrage balloons. The newspaper declared that it was published "by and for the men and officers of the Barrage Balloon Training Center, Camp Tyson, Tennessee." Here is the front page for the August 19, 1942, edition, which tells about General Maynard dedicating the USO (for the white soldiers) in Paris. Several old issues reveal that the *Gas Bag* did cover the activities of both the black and white soldiers at the camp. (Author's collection.)

Camp Tyson was so large that it required two fire departments, one on either side of the camp. Here are two members of one of the fire departments with one of their water trucks. In the background is one of the churches. (Courtesy of Wayne Webb.)

Two officers pose in front of a map of Europe in the War Information Office at the camp. The photograph is stamped on the back "*Gas Bag*," indicating it was used by the camp newsletter.

(Courtesy of Wayne Webb.)

The US Army Signal Corps took this photograph of camp commander Col. Frederick B. Dodge, at left, and Cpl. John W. Leonard shaking hands. The US Signal Corps photographs were used for publicity purposes and were sent to newspapers around the country as well the *Gas Bag*. (Courtesy of Wayne Webb.)

The men of Camp Tyson Fire Station No. 2 line up for a photograph. Local civilians worked as firefighters for the two Camp Tyson fire stations. This 1944 photograph shows, from left to right, Hubert Hooper, Joe Moser, Eldrigh Cathey, Pape Tucker, Harry Hicks, Richard Crank, unidentified, and Bill Argo. (Courtesy of Brenda Lewis.)

Five WACs pose in front of an inflated barrage balloon. The WACs had their own quarters, officers, and duties at Camp Tyson, but unfortunately, little documentation of their activities remains today. Even photographs of the WACs at Camp Tyson are rare. (Courtesy of Wayne Webb.)

This is a Signal Corps photograph of Capt. Irene L. Miller at her desk at Camp Tyson. The WACs were not trained in the operation of the barrage balloons. (Courtesy of Wayne Webb.)

Six

Romance of the Barrage Balloons

Henry Countians were fascinated by the barrage balloons that dotted their skies all day and often into the evenings.

Farmers like Frank Brown would stop what they were doing and sit a while on their tractors, looking at the giant balloons. "That was quite a sight for a country boy like me," Brown said.

Children like Mary Alice Burton Campbell and Jeannette McFarlin would gather in their front yards on Park Street in Paris after school, counting how many balloons each saw. "The funny thing was, nobody ever got the same count, so we'd all have to start counting again," McFarlin remembered.

But what really got everyone's attention was when the balloons would get loose.

During training at Camp Tyson, barrage balloons would sometimes become dislodged and float aimlessly over the countryside. William Crosser remembered many times watching soldiers in their jeeps chasing the balloons, waiting for the helium to run out and the balloons to fall to earth.

Balloons landed far and wide—much farther than one might think. Barrage balloons from Camp Tyson were reported as far away as Proctor, North Carolina; Camp Campbell, Kentucky (now Fort Campbell); Frenchmans Bayou, Arkansas; Pulaski, Alabama; and several towns in Tennessee and Mississippi. The *Gas Bag* used to report on the runaway balloons and the endeavors of the soldiers in catching them with much humor.

Former soldier Loyal Whiteside of Florida kept a scrapbook that includes a newspaper article reporting a runaway balloon that landed near New Corydon, Indiana. According to the article, a detail of 25 soldiers was sent to recover the balloon, driving all night to find the balloon hanging in a tree.

Nelda Pinson of Paris remembered, as a child at the tiny VanDyke school, when a balloon came down in the nearby field. Her teacher decided to turn the spectacle into a learning experience, using it as a field trip with the children eating their lunch and watching the soldiers retrieve it.

A telegram sent to Camp Tyson on June 9, 1943, reported that some citizens took rather drastic action to take down a wayward balloon. The telegram reported, "Barrage balloon which broke loose from mooring at Camp Tyson shot down over Lake Erie returned to Akron for repairs, General Tire and Rubber Co."

Barrage balloons are tethered to the ground at Camp Tyson, with weights attached to keep them from flying off. Despite such precautions, barrage balloons did occasionally fly away from the camp, often landing in nearby farm fields. They also landed much farther away, as happened in October 1943, when a runaway balloon interfered with an American Airlines plane, causing a crash near Nashville that killed 10 people, including Blan Maxwell, the lieutenant governor of Tennessee. This photograph, taken in 1943, was made into a postcard that was sold at the Camp Tyson PX. (Courtesy of Lou and Bettye Carter.)

Camp Tyson soldiers worked for hours on training exercises, both at the camp and outside locations, such as on barges at the nearby Kentucky Lake and on training trips across the state and the region. In this photograph included in the 306th Coast Artillery yearbook, soldiers inflate a barrage balloon at the camp during maneuvers. (Author's collection.)

This is as up close and personal to a barrage balloon as anyone living today can get. Barrage balloons came in different sizes and configurations. Some looked more like blimps, while others resembled airplanes, but each type was designed with maximum aerodynamics in mind. The huge balloons were designed so they could be tethered to the ground or flown from warships. (Courtesy of Wayne Webb.)

Paul Soik was the artist who painted *Haul 'Er Down* (page 88). Soik, of Lyndhurst, New Jersey, continued his war experiences after Camp Tyson. He joined the 11th Airborne Division as a paratrooper, serving in the Philippines. In a letter to Roland Parkhill of Paris, he said, "We were the first troops to enter Japan on V-J Day." Soik did numerous pencil sketches of the aftermath of one of the atomic bombs while in Japan. (Courtesy of Roland Parkhill.)

Thanks to Roland Parkhill of Paris, *Haul 'Er Down* has been preserved and is on permanent display at the Paris–Henry County Heritage Center. Parkhill is also responsible for preserving the story behind the painting. Paul Soik painted it while a soldier at the camp. Soik later became a nationally known graphic artist. The painting had been kept at the camp and was found by Parkhill in the 1990s. Parkhill had it restored and tracked down Soik, who thought the painting was lost. The two began a correspondence that lasted until Soik died in 2000. (Courtesy of Paris–Henry County Heritage Center.)

Seven

Finding Comfort

To combat the routine and drudgery involved with Army life, the War Department went out of its way to improve the morale of its soldiers as much as possible. And that was as true for the Camp Tyson soldiers as for any. Camp Tyson may have been way out of the way, but that didn't mean that big-time entertainment passed it by.

The camp's Service Club and both of its USOs (for white and black soldiers) attracted plenty of entertainment, including song and dance star Eddie Bracken, magicians, dancing girls, comedians, and others, but the biggest star to arrive at Camp Tyson by far was Jeanette MacDonald.

MacDonald was a star of stage and screen, and people in Paris can still vividly describe her glowing blond hair as she arrived on the *Pan-American* at the Louisville & Nashville train depot for her appearance on August 1, 1942.

It was pouring rain, but that did not stop crowds from awaiting her arrival. It did, however, play havoc on her performance, in which she sang in the dark as the electricity kept going on and off.

The town was abuzz, and a suitable location had to be found for the movie star to stay. The former Laureighn Hotel was selected by the camp officers, and a local newspaper reported on how much hotel owner Laureighn Copeland worked to get her rooms ship-shape for the visit. Copeland couldn't believe that MacDonald traveled with such a large entourage. "Why, she wanted a suite of rooms," she said, adding that the switchboard was ringing off the wall.

During her visit, MacDonald visited several downtown stores, ate at the Plaza Café, and posed—without her stage makeup—in front of the former Humphreys Café on Brewer Street.

But she really charmed everyone by making a special visit at the request of a soldier at a camp in California, who asked her to deliver a message to his sweetheart, Ruth Humphreys, who lived in Paris. She delivered the message personally. After finding that Ruth worked for her brother, Dr. K.B. Humphreys Sr., in the Commercial Bank Building, Jeanette MacDonald surprised Ruth by popping into the office with the message. The local newspaper, in an understatement, reported that Ruth was "thrilled."

While in Paris for her appearance at Camp Tyson, movie star Jeannette MacDonald poses for a photograph (without makeup and in her casual clothes) in front of the former Humphrey's Café, which was at the corner of Brewer and East Wood Streets. (Courtesy of Wayne Webb.)

An unidentified woman poses at the outdoor amphitheater on the camp's grounds. Camp Tyson boasted a wide variety of entertainment venues for soldiers and their guests, and the amphitheater was used as a venue for skits and band performances during the warm-weather months. (Courtesy of Wayne Webb.)

The Service Club was the scene of many festive and sentimental evenings at the camp. The club was a popular destination for local girls, who were strictly chaperoned by matrons hired by the camp. Here, local girls in fancy gowns and soldiers are pictured at a New Year's Eve celebration. (Courtesy of Wayne Webb.)

Another view of the interior of the Service Club depicts a formal dinner involving male officers and their wives at the head table, along with another group of male and female officers. (Courtesy of Wayne Webb.)

One of the largest buildings on the camp was the Service Club. It was an active spot and the scene of a variety of events. Many dances and dinners were held at the club, and many wartime romances were kindled there. The weekly dances were heavily chaperoned, and girls from Paris were told ahead of time that proper decorum was required of them. (Courtesy of Wayne Webb.)

The Camp Tyson band performs at evening retreat in this undated photograph that was included in the 306th Coast Artillery yearbook. By all accounts, Camp Tyson had an exemplary band, and the band director, Tom Lonardo, was one of many Camp Tyson soldiers who married local women and stayed in Paris. Lonardo owned and operated the Lonardo Music Store in Paris for decades and was director of a popular band that performed swing music in West Tennessee. (Author's collection.)

All work and no play would make for dull Army life. That could be what was on the mind of this officer, photographed taking his best golf swing while others wait their turn at the officers' golf course on the camp. According to *Remembering Camp Tyson*, by Herston Cooper, the photographer reported: "The ball whizzed away for 40 inches—give or take a few inches." (Courtesy of Wayne Webb.)

Two nurses and a soldier are pictured with baby foxes found at the camp. The mother fox built a den under the dispensary, and the nurses started feeding them. Before long, the foxes were their pets. This photograph was used in the *Gas Bag* and for publicity purposes. (Courtesy of Wayne Webb.)

Eight

Soldiers Segregated

Like the rest of the South during World War II and beyond, Henry County was segregated, which made wartime for the African American soldiers and their families especially difficult.

Likewise, Camp Tyson was segregated, with black and white soldiers housed in different areas. Three African American battalions were stationed at Camp Tyson during the war (the 318th, 319th, and the 320th), and their training was largely segregated.

Black soldiers from the north, especially from the urban areas, were uncomfortable with the outright segregation prevalent in the camp and in Henry County.

The USOs were separate, with the black soldiers welcomed at their USO on Rison Street (a large white auditorium that still stands) and the white soldiers at their USO at the corner of Brewer and Washington Streets in Paris. The families of black soldiers also had separate quarters at the camp when they came to visit.

There were plenty of establishments for the black soldiers to enjoy, such as the Tip Top Café on West Blythe Street in Paris, where the waitresses wore white gloves and fancy little white hats. The local black churches also opened their arms to the soldiers, inviting them for luncheons and get-togethers. And the *Gas Bag* did publish columns on the goings-on of the African American battalions during their leisure time.

Sgt. George Davison wrote down his memories of his Camp Tyson days and said, "Colored troops had it hard back then." He remembered an ugly incident that involved black soldiers being barred from a Paris drugstore until their white commander, Col. Leon Reed, insisted they be allowed in.

The ugliest incident of all, of course, was the still unsolved murder on July 31, 1943, of Pvt. Herman Hankins of Danville, Virginia, who is today buried in an unmarked grave in the black section of Maplewood Cemetery in Paris. Hankins was accused of being a peeping tom and was shot and killed by white soldiers in a tourist camp in Routon. But soldiers who knew him, including Wilson Monk, never believed that. Monk was at the grave and took a photograph that he still keeps. Hankins was a member of the 320th. "I don't believe what Herman was accused of," Monk said. "He wasn't that kind of guy."

Bill Davison, of Waynesburg, Pennsylvania, has kept alive the memory of the 320th Barrage Balloon Battalion and his father, George, all these years. George Davison kept memorabilia from his time at Camp Tyson and with the 320th, including newspaper articles, ticket stubs, and banners. But he also wrote down his memories, which his son found after George's death in 2002 and memorialized on a website he created. "I wanted to make sure these men were not forgotten," Bill said. Here is his father, looking very sharp in his uniform. (Courtesy of Bill Davison.)

Sgt. George A. Davison and other members of the 320th Anti-Aircraft Barrage Balloon Battalion surround a farmhouse near Vierville-sur-Mer, Normandy, as they search for German snipers in June 1944. The 320th was the only all-black battalion to participate in the D-Day invasion. (Courtesy of Bill Davison.)

One of the more iconic photographs from World War II was taken during the D-Day invasion. Note the barrage balloons hovering overhead. Men from the 320th trained at Camp Tyson were operating the balloons. (Courtesy of the Library of Congress.)

Well-dressed Parisians line the streets around the court square as African American soldiers participate in the parade of Camp Tyson vehicles and barrage balloons. The US Army and officers at Camp Tyson went out of their way to become part of the local community, and parades in downtown Paris were a part of that endeavor. (Courtesy of Virgil Wall.)

Soldiers salute as they parade by Camp Tyson officers. Despite the segregation of black and white soldiers at the camp, both are marching together. (Courtesy of Wayne Webb.)

Waverly Woodson was one of the members of the 320th Anti-Aircraft Balloon Barrage Battalion who saw combat on D-Day. He was among the men whose job it was to secure the barrage balloons along the coastline to block the view from German gunners. He was 21 at the time. He died in 2005. His archives were donated by his descendants to the Langston Hughes Memorial Library Special Collections at Lincoln University. (Courtesy of Lincoln University.)

Many Henry County marriages began at Camp Tyson as soldiers decided to settle down with the girls they met while at the camp. One man who did just that was S.Sgt. Oscar Gardner, who fell in love with Mary Will while she was working at the black soldiers' USO. Their marriage endured all their lives. (Courtesy of Mary Will Gardner.)

It was a lucky day for the black community in Paris when Joseph Harden was assigned to Camp Tyson. Hailing from Rome, Georgia, Harden met Elizabeth Diggs of Paris while he was stationed at the camp, and together the couple became central figures in the education of generations of young people. Harden was principal at the former Henry County Training School, and his wife taught elementary school there for many years. After schools were integrated in Paris, Harden was appointed assistant superintendent and supervisor of guidance and attendance for the Paris school district. (Courtesy of Nona Moore.)

Joseph Harden (standing, center) and his wife, the former Elizabeth Diggs (seated, far right), are pictured with the faculty of the former Henry County Training School. Also pictured is Mary Will Gardner (standing, far left), a Paris girl who also met and married a Camp Tyson soldier, Oscar Gardner. (Courtesy of Mary Will Gardner.)

Although African American soldiers were housed at Camp Tyson, their quarters—and their lives—were separate from the white soldiers. A separate USO served them, and they also found other venues for entertainment during their off-duty hours away from those of the white soldiers. One such spot was the Tip Top Café, a fancy establishment at 418 West Blythe Street where waitresses dressed in uniforms. In this photograph, several military police from the camp are visiting the Tip Top. Roland Atkinson waited tables there and said it was "a hopping place." The tall MP second from left is Lieutenant Peterson. The waitress at right is Maude T. Sutton. (Courtesy of Roland Atkinson.)

One of the outlets available for relaxation for African American soldiers at Camp Tyson was a visit to a local church. Often, soldiers performed at church picnics and church services. Here are the Deuces at a gathering at Barrs Chapel African Methodist Episcopalian Church outside of Paris. (Courtesy of Dorothy Cook.)

In this undated photograph, the Quinn Chapel AME Church in Paris hosts a group of soldiers for a celebration. Note the two soldiers seated on the right holding up their fingers in a victory sign. The photograph still hangs at the church. (Courtesy of Quinn Chapel AME Church.)

Soldiers from the three African American battalions marched in the parades in nearby towns; this photograph was taken around the Paris court square. (Courtesy of Wayne Webb.)

This close-up of a parade through downtown Paris shows black and white soldiers marching together. This is rather remarkable for the time, considering that Camp Tyson, like all Southern military camps, was segregated. (Courtesy of Wayne Webb.)

Nine

Preparing for the End

Camp Tyson received official notification that it would be disbanded on April 20, 1945. The camp commander was informed that all troops still housed there would be relocated.

This was several months before the official end of World War II, but behind-the-scenes plans had actually been in place for the camp's closure after the D-Day landing on June 6, 1944. By that time, barrage balloons were considered obsolete, and Camp Tyson's usefulness was coming to a close.

Toward the end of the war, Camp Tyson became a staging area for soldiers who would be transferred to locations overseas.

It was a sad time for Henry Countians and for Camp Tyson. The excitement that surrounded the camp was coming to an end.

But beyond the sadness came anger in the weeks and months ahead as the government made decisions that were considered wasteful to many Henry Countians. In a time when the South was still pulling itself out of economic bad times, many of the hundreds of buildings were either sold for scrap or just bulldozed. Caches of food and inventory—which could have been utilized by local residents—were instead buried on the grounds.

Bennye Phillips of Hazel, Kentucky, whose father was hired as an overseer of the camp during its final days, said her father salvaged as much as he could because he was so upset at the waste he was witnessing. Her dad, Claude Barber White Sr., told her the camp "was just dumping things out over there."

Those who were especially angered were the families whose homes had been acquired for Camp Tyson by eminent domain. Members of the Steele and Lankford families recalled that the government had bulldozed their homes and set fire to their crops with very little notice so that the camp could be built. To have the camp close after such a short time was especially galling.

Jeanne Townsend of Paris had worked as a secretary for several officers, and was among those who worked on the camp's final day. She said, "We were the last people to leave when the camp closed. I remember we put a black wreath on the gate at the camp as we left."

On Camp Tyson's last day of operation, employees and their bosses gather for one last photograph. From left to right are Lyndon Shelton of Fayetteville, Jeanne Anderson Townsend, an unidentified soldier, Mary Joe Burke Wyatt of Murphysboro, and Private First Class Grissom. (Courtesy of Jeanne Townsend.)

Unidentified employees of Camp Tyson are seen here on the camp's last day. With a black wreath on the door, they pose with handkerchiefs at their faces. (Courtesy of Wayne Webb.)

After the camp was closed, the old entrances started looking the worse for wear. This was one of the back entrances to the camp in the days after the war. (Courtesy of Wayne Webb.)

Ten

Life after Camp Tyson

Late in the war, Camp Tyson was used as a prisoner of war camp for Italian and German soldiers, who were placed in the camp's stockade.

The government began selling some land back to the original owners, and for a time, the camp became a ghost town as local newspapers began publicly asking what would happen to the facility, its grounds, and the local economy.

The government advertised for bids for the property, and two bidders emerged: the Spinks Clay Company and the Young Business Men's Club of Paris.

With its government contacts and a full business plan, the Spinks Clay Company eventually emerged as the new owner. A large-scale ball clay business and cattle farm owned by the Carothers family already operated businesses in nearby counties and owned the area mineral and mining rights. After much haggling, the final price paid by Spinks was $201,000.

Over the next decades, the Spinks Clay Company maintained both the clay business and a cattle ranch at the Camp Tyson property, utilizing the offices, motor pools, streets, and 90-foot hangar (used for sorting clay by the new owners). The business employed hundreds of people, including a large group of cowboys for the ranch. Employees lived on the grounds in former barracks converted to apartments. The Carothers family also lived on the grounds in former barracks. Richard Sr. and his wife, Harriet, lived in the former general's home, which was more often than not overrun by cattle.

Family members and employees alike remembered the arrangement with fondness—it was almost idyllic in their view.

Today, the Belgium-based Lhoist Spinks Company owns the property, and most of the old streets are covered over in weeds. But the cattle still roam free.

FOR SALE OR LEASE
FACTORY SITES
WITH IMPROVEMENTS

Desirable Industrial Sites Suitable For:—
Light Manufacturing, Warehousing and Storage
Together With Many Other Possibilities.

LOCATED AT PARIS, TENNESSEE

KNOWN AS

Camp Tyson Military Reservation (For Sale or Lease in Place as a Whole or in Separate Real Estate Units, Also Sewage Disposal Plant and Incinerator.)

LOCATION

In the midst of the Industrial Tennessee Valley, approximately five miles Southwest of Paris, Henry County, Tennessee, adjacent to U. S. Highway No. 79 and served by the L. & N. Railroad.

SITE AS A WHOLE

The entire site comprises approximately 1,298.9 acres with the following improvements, water mains, sewers, incinerator, sewage disposal plant, railroad sidings, adequate phone facilities, network of hard surfaced roads, electrical distribution system, deep wells, pumping stations and water treatment plant, approximately 500,000 gallon elevated steel water tank, steel balloon hangar, with two (2) H.P. Line Pressure boilers and steam heating system with radiators and blowers, approximately one quarter million square feet of warehousing space, together with other buildings and improvements.

REAL ESTATE UNITS

Unit No. 1

Approximately 275 acres together with approximately 13 buildings of various sizes and types of wood and masonry construction. Building and improvements can be identified by the following numbers: 615, 694, 696, 697, 699, 785, 1450, 1451, 1452, 1453, 1454, 1455, and 1456.

Unit No. 2

Approximately 355 acres together with approximately 36 buildings of various sizes and types of wood and masonry construction. Buildings and improvements can be identified by the following numbers: 8, 9, 10, 11, 12, 13, 14, 15, 16, 17, 18, 23, 24, 32, 33, 46, 47, 56, 64, 65, 66, 67, 83, 85, 86, 100, 110, 117, 123, 134, 136, 138, 608, 1095 and 1230.

Unit No. 3

Approximately 390 acres together with approximately 37 buildings of various sizes and types of wood and masonry construction. Buildings and improvements can be identified by the following numbers: 813, 815, 816, 817, 818, 875, 876, 1105, 1106, 1107, 1114, 1125, 1130, 1150, 1151, 1153, 1154, 1155, 1157, 1160, 1161, 1162, 1163, 1167, 1168, 1171, 1172, 1173, 1174, 1175, 1180, 1181, 1221, 1222, 1223, 1237, and 1251.

Unit No. 4

After the US government decided to designate the camp as surplus, ads began appearing in local newspapers in an attempt to sell the camp and its contents. (Courtesy of Rebecca Goins.)

After Camp Tyson was declared surplus by the government, it was purchased in May 1947 by the H.C. Spinks Clay Company, a partnership owned by R.B. Carothers Sr., Harriett Carothers, R.B. Carothers Jr., and Harry S. Carothers. Harriett's nickname was "Josie," and her maiden name was Spinks. They purchased approximately 1,300 acres from war assets. After the purchase of the property, H.C. Spinks's headquarters was moved from Northern Kentucky to the former Camp Tyson. Here, heavy machinery is used to dig the first clay pits at the former Army camp. (Courtesy of the Carothers family.)

Members of the Carothers family are pictured in the early years, after they had first purchased Camp Tyson, posing by the headquarters building. At far left in the first row is Rich Carothers standing next to his parents, Josie and Richard Carothers. (Courtesy of Wayne Webb.)

A working ranch with cattle and horses was situated at the former Camp Tyson grounds after the war was over, and among the dozens of cowboys who worked there was Shorty Hutcherson of Paris, at right. Hutcherson still recalls his days working on the ranch fondly. (Courtesy of the Carothers family.)

The massive size of the 90-foot hangar can clearly be seen in this photograph, taken in the 1940s after the Carothers family acquired the camp property. The main offices are dwarfed by the hangar. The Spinks Clay Company offices were converted from the camp headquarters. Both of these buildings are still used by the Lhoist Spinks Clay Company. (Courtesy of the Carothers family.)

The Carothers family lived in the barracks that formerly housed Camp Tyson commander Gen. John Maynard on the grounds. In this photograph taken in October 1947, one can see how rustic the surroundings were. (Courtesy of the Carothers family.)

This is another view of the home the Carothers family fashioned for themselves from a former barracks. As can be seen, the barracks could be renovated to create nice housing. Former employees of the Spinks Company who also lived in the barracks reported that the homes were very comfortable. Some of the barracks were so large that they could be divided into apartments. (Courtesy of the Carothers family.)

After the Spinks Company purchased the former Camp Tyson, company officials used every building and bit of machinery that had not been destroyed by the Army. That included old Quonset huts such as this one, which was converted into a barn. (Courtesy of the Carothers family.)

Spinks Clay Company owner Dick Carothers Sr., right, is pictured with a customer after the Spinks Company had located at the former camp. It is interesting to note that the photograph was taken by Val Umbach, a Camp Tyson soldier who settled in Paris after marrying a local girl, Christine Reynolds. Umbach was from Chicago and was assigned to one of the early units that organized Camp Tyson. Umbach turned his interest in photography into a business that endured for decades in Paris, so much so that the Umbach name became synonymous with photography in the area. Umbach was also a musician and sang at weddings. Many in Paris tell stories about Umbach singing at their wedding and then jumping down into the aisles to take photographs. (Courtesy of the Carothers family.)

Dick Carothers Sr. looks over some cattle on the property. (Courtesy of the Carothers family.)

As at any other ranch, branding of cattle was a regular occurrence at the Carothers ranch after the war, as can be seen in this March 1947 photograph. Employees at the Spinks Clay Company enjoyed their close proximity to the cattle and horse ranch on the grounds, including Carl Ross Veazey, who said he liked to take breaks and watch the action at the ranch. (Courtesy of the Carothers family.)

Earl McCree, left, and two other Spinks ranch employees are hard at work gathering hay for the cattle and horses. (Courtesy of the Carothers family.)

Rich Carothers works a tractor on the ranch at the old Camp Tyson grounds in April 1948. (Courtesy of the Carothers family.)

Mary Jeffers and Bob Klocke oversee work at the Humphreys pit, which was being constructed in September 1947. Unusually for the time, the Carothers family employed several women in supervisory roles. (Courtesy of the Carothers family.)

The Bowdens were longtime employees of the Carothers cattle and horse ranches. Here, Pete Bowden is showing one of the horses for the photographer in 1947. (Courtesy of the Carothers family.)

Old barracks were converted to homes or apartments for employees and family members and remained on the grounds, where employees could be close to their work. The barracks homes were provided to employees with no rent or utilities charged. Here is one of the old barracks after it was split into apartments in June 1947. (Courtesy of the Carothers family.)

Among those who lived in the old barracks were Carothers family members. Here is a November 1947 photograph of Rich Carothers, his wife, Margie, and their son, Skip, at their barracks apartment. (Courtesy of the Carothers family.)

The old 90-foot hangar was used by the Spinks Clay Company for sorting clay, and it is still used by the Lhoist Spinks Clay Company. This photograph was taken in April 1948. (Courtesy of the Carothers family.)

Charlie McClure, left, and Rich Carothers pose in front of McClure's office at the Spinks Clay Company. The Spinks offices were located in the former Camp Tyson offices. McClure was a longtime employee at Spinks, and as a history lover, he wrote a three-page history of Camp Tyson that has been preserved by Spinks employees. McClure worked there from 1947 to 1997. His office was memorialized with a plaque reading "Charlie's Place" above the office door, with his dates of employment. (Courtesy of Ralph Anderson.)

Workers pour the foundation for the clay dryer oil tanks in October 1947. The former camp was an especially busy place in the days and weeks after the Carothers family purchased the grounds and set about transforming it into a clay company. (Courtesy of the Carothers family.)

The Carothers family utilized as much of the former Camp Tyson equipment and buildings as they could. The 90-foot hangar was converted for use by the Spinks Clay Company, and these are the dryer and furnace that were installed in October 1947. (Courtesy of the Carothers family.)

Don Bowden poses with a little boy on one of the many horses at the Carothers ranch after the war. (Courtesy of the Carothers family.)

In addition to the Spinks Clay Company and the cattle and horse ranch that were located at the former Camp Tyson, the Carothers family also held fox hunts on the property for several years in the 1940s. Here are several men gathered with Richard Carothers (standing, far left) for a fox hunt in January 1948 along with their hunting dogs. (Courtesy of the Carothers family.)

One of the Carothers family's favorite horses was named Coke McCue, and this April 1944 photograph of him is one of many the family took. None of the family members today know why he had such an exotic name. (Courtesy of the Carothers family.)

For the Carothers family, showing and selling the horses from their ranch was big business. Here is the cover of a program that was used for the 11th annual sale at the H.C. Spinks Farms and Ranches on August 1, 1964. The brochures included several pages of photographs and descriptions of the horses that were for sale. (Courtesy of Ralph Anderson.)

Richard Carothers—called "Mr. Dick" by his employees and friends—poses with one of his favorite horses, Cow Lady. The photograph was used in one of the Spinks Ranch brochures. (Courtesy of the Carothers family.)

Joe Lankford points out one of several tie-downs used to secure barrage balloons that remain on his Steele Road farm. Other remnants of the camp can be found on farms on or near where the camp was located, including the cement bases used for the barrage balloons. Lankford's family is one of those that bought back land that was taken by the government to build the camp. (Author's collection.)

Work at the Spinks Clay Company was always hard. Here, a worker unloads clay from a front loader on the grounds. (Courtesy of the Carothers family.)

Men working at the former Spinks cattle and horse ranch pause briefly for a photograph. From all reports, working at the ranch on the Spinks property was a good—and actually pretty glamorous—job. (Author's collection.)

There still are many remnants of the camp on the grounds today. The old furnace still stands, but it is no longer used. (Author's collection.)

The Lhoist Spinks Company still uses the old Camp Tyson offices. The interior of the offices has been remodeled and now contains laboratories for the clay company. (Author's collection.)

The old motor pool from Camp Tyson is still used as a garage by the clay company and is one of the busiest buildings on the grounds. (Author's collection.)

One can still find plenty of reminders of the Spinks Clay Company and Camp Tyson on the grounds. The company still uses the facilities that were constructed long ago. (Author's collection.)

A sign welcomes visitors to the Lhoist North America Spinks Clay Company in Routon today. The company is now owned by a Belgium-based international firm, but the new owners still honor its roots by calling it the Camp Tyson Plant. (Author's collection.)

The State of Tennessee placed a historical marker near the entrance of the former Camp Tyson commemorating its place in history. (Author's collection.)

Today, the land where Camp Tyson once stood is still used for farming, but instead of the Carothers family overseeing the old ranch and farm, the Lhoist Spinks Clay Company contracts the land to local farmers. (Author's collection.)